$2.50

HOFFNUNG'S MUSICAL CHAIRS

By the Author of
THE MAESTRO
THE HOFFNUNG SYMPHONY ORCHESTRA
THE HOFFNUNG MUSIC FESTIVAL
THE HOFFNUNG COMPANION TO MUSIC
HOFFNUNG'S ACOUSTICS

Hoffnung's Musical Chairs

By
Gerard
Hoffnung

SOUVENIR PRESS

Copyright © 1958 Gerard Hoffnung

First published 1958 by Dennis Dobson

This edition first published 1983 by Souvenir Press Ltd, 43 Great Russell Street, London WC1B 3PA

Reprinted November 1983
Reprinted October 1985

All Rights Reserved. No part of this publication may be reproduced, stored in a retrieval system, or transmitted, in any form or by any means, electronic, mechanical, photocopying, recording or otherwise without the prior permission of the copyright owner

ISBN 0 285 62612 4

I am obliged, as ever, to Messrs Bradbury, Agnew & Co Ltd, for allowing me to include drawings in this volume which originally appeared in Punch.

For

MALCOLM ARNOLD

Printed in Great Britain by
Photobooks (Bristol) Ltd.

Carnival of Animals

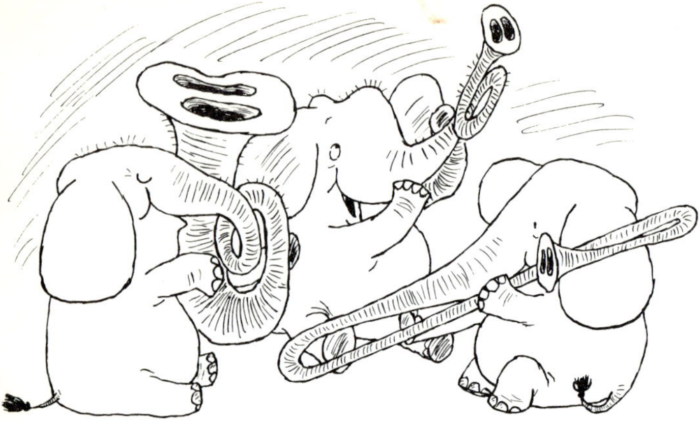

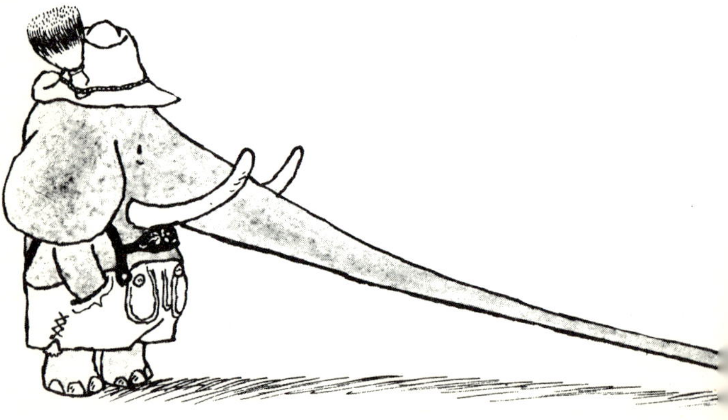

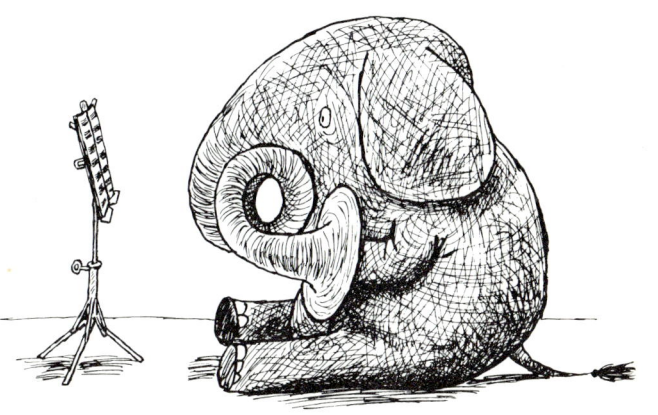

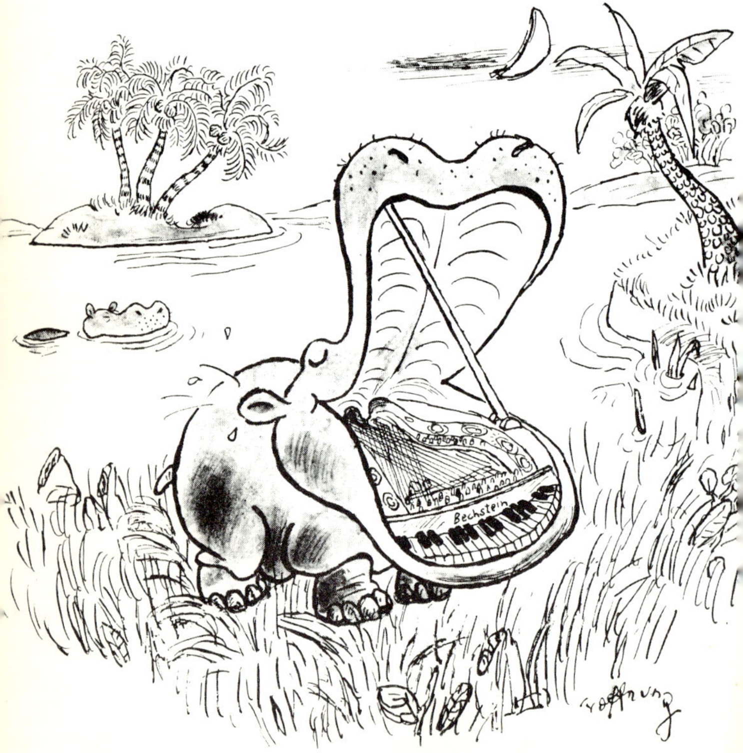
Bechstein

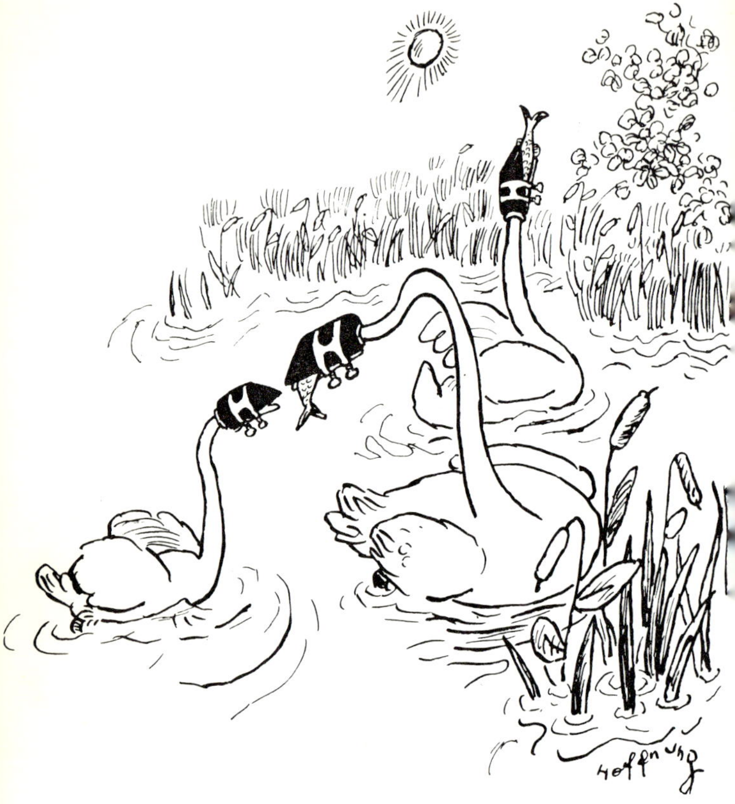
Hoffnung

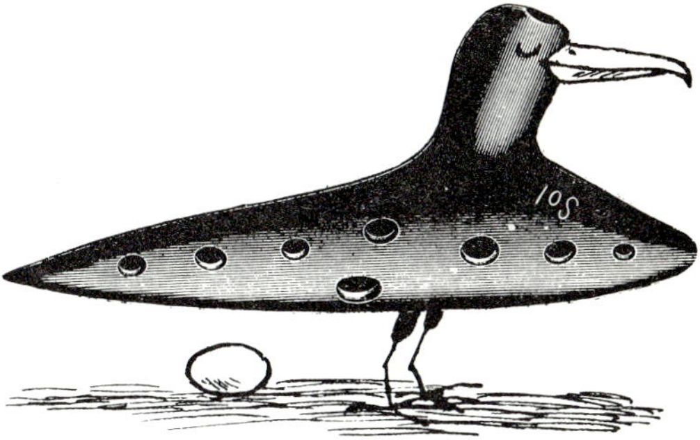

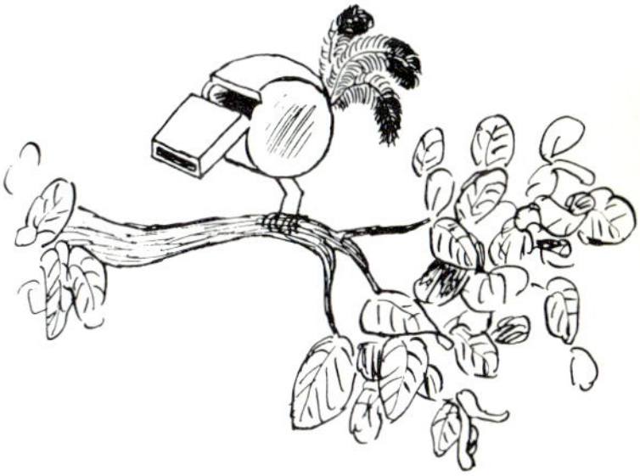

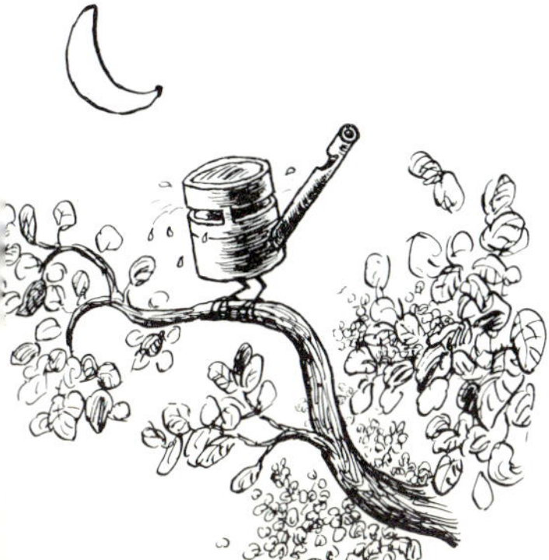

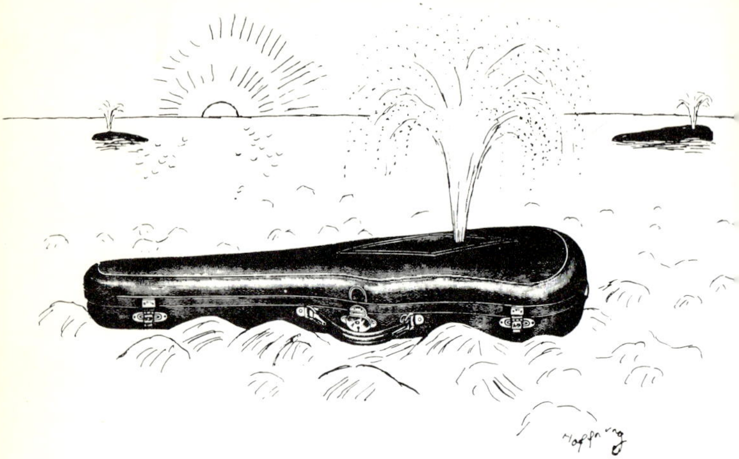
Hoffnung

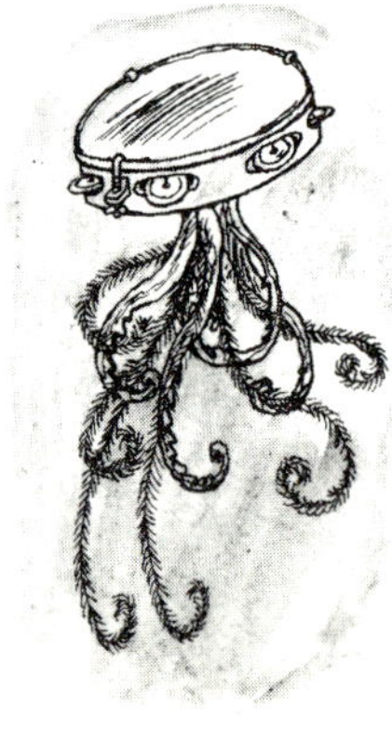

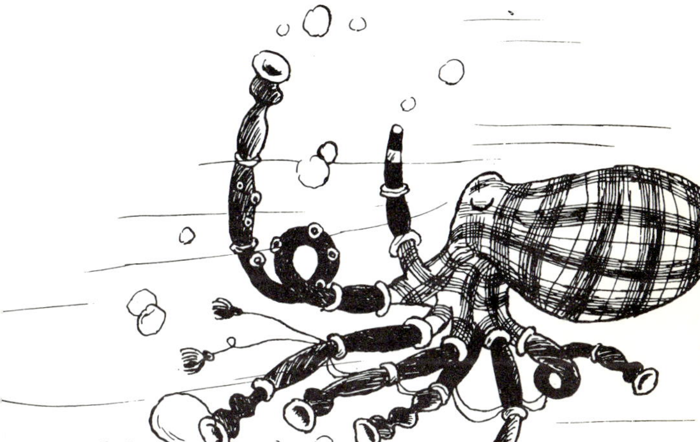

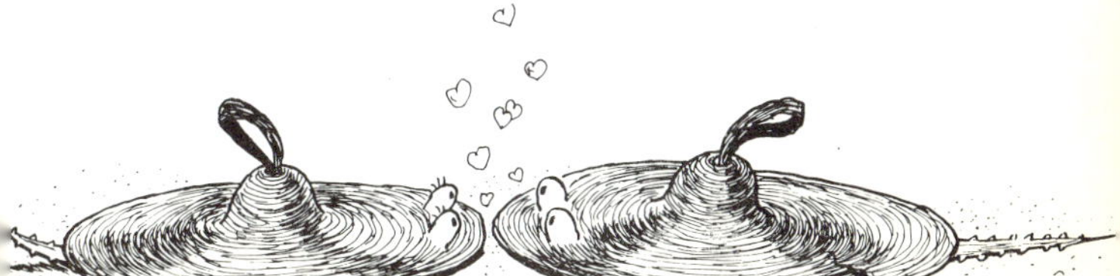

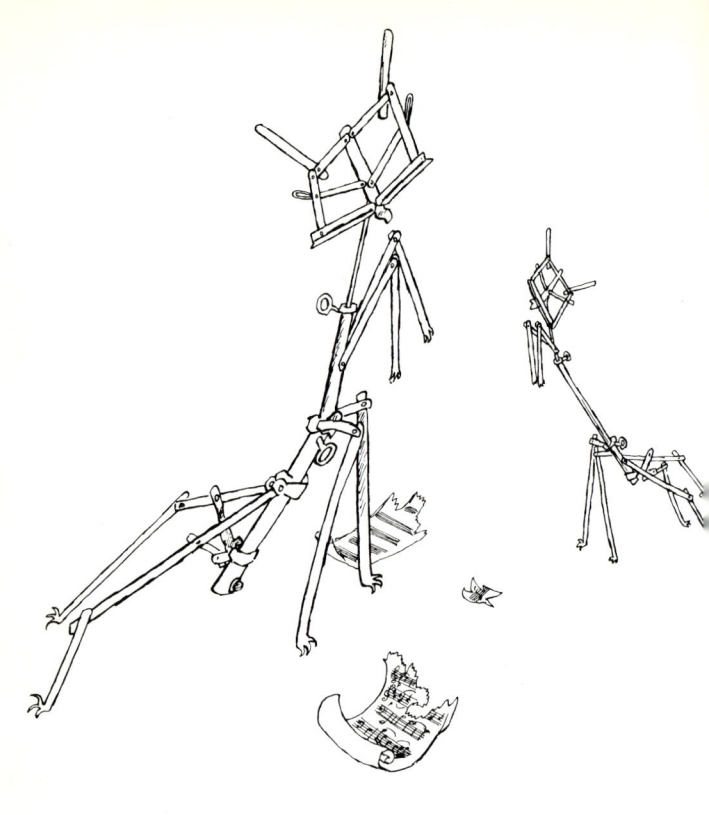

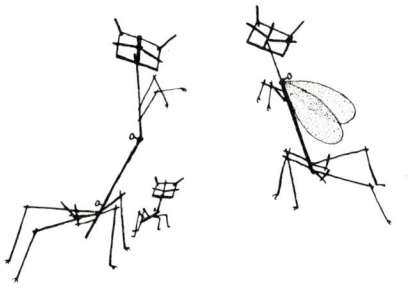

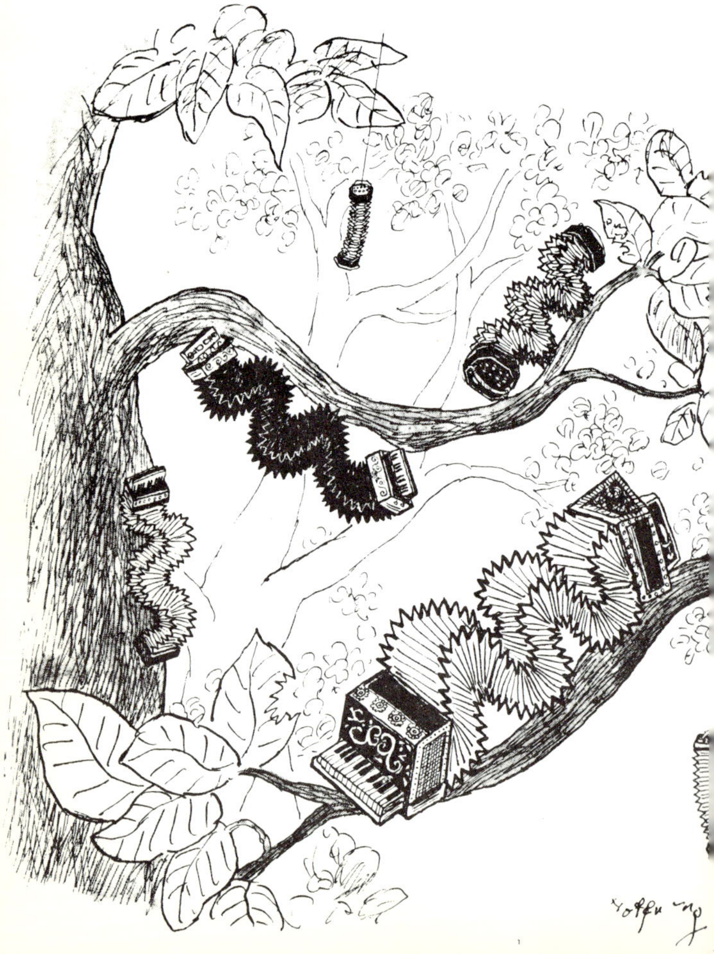

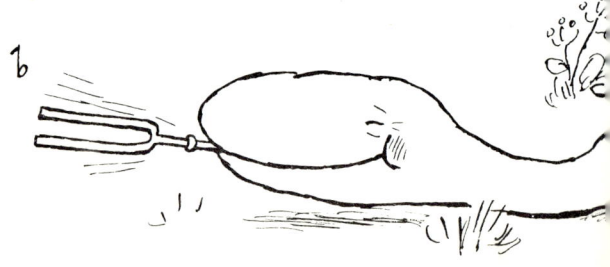

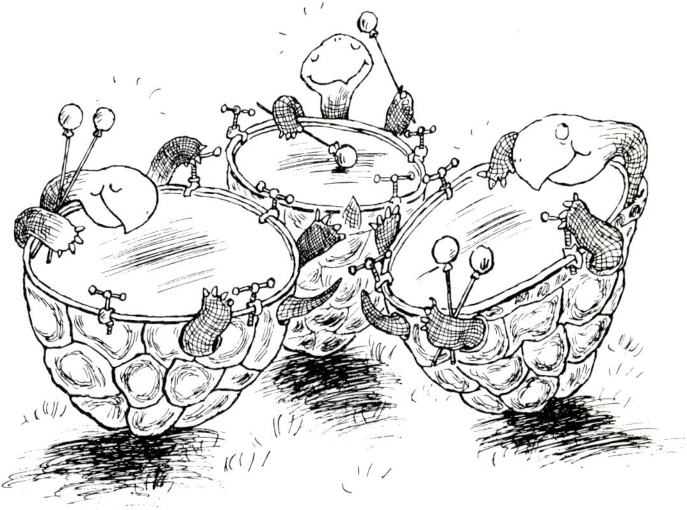

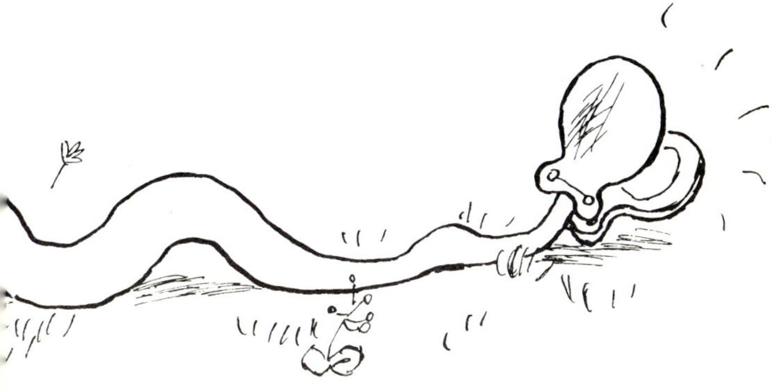

Light Cavalry

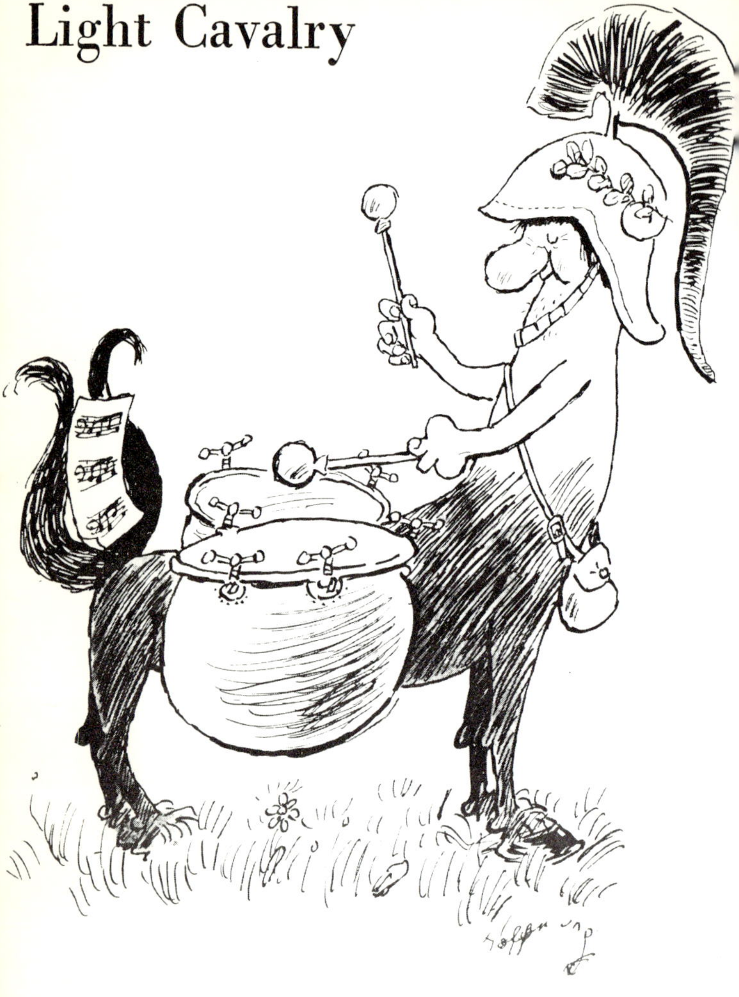

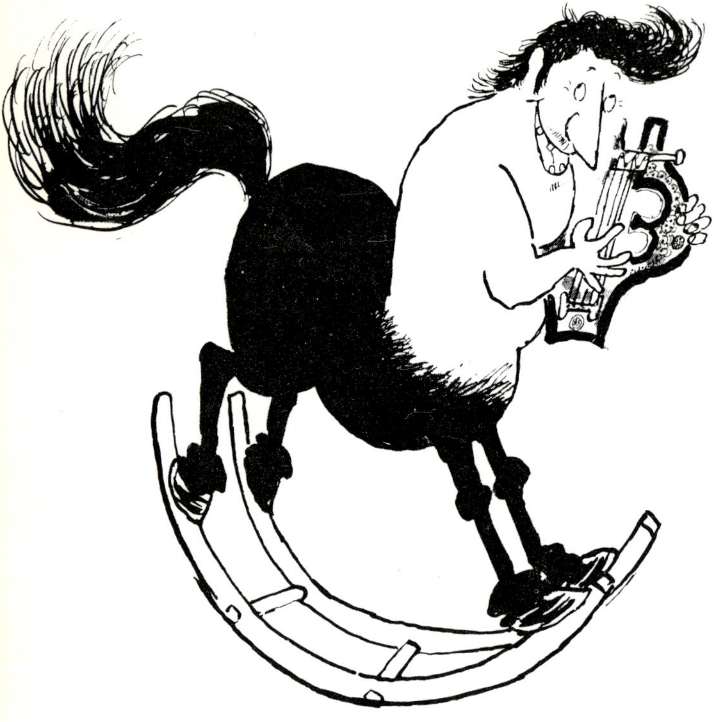

Early outbreaks of Rock 'n Roll

Rites of Spring

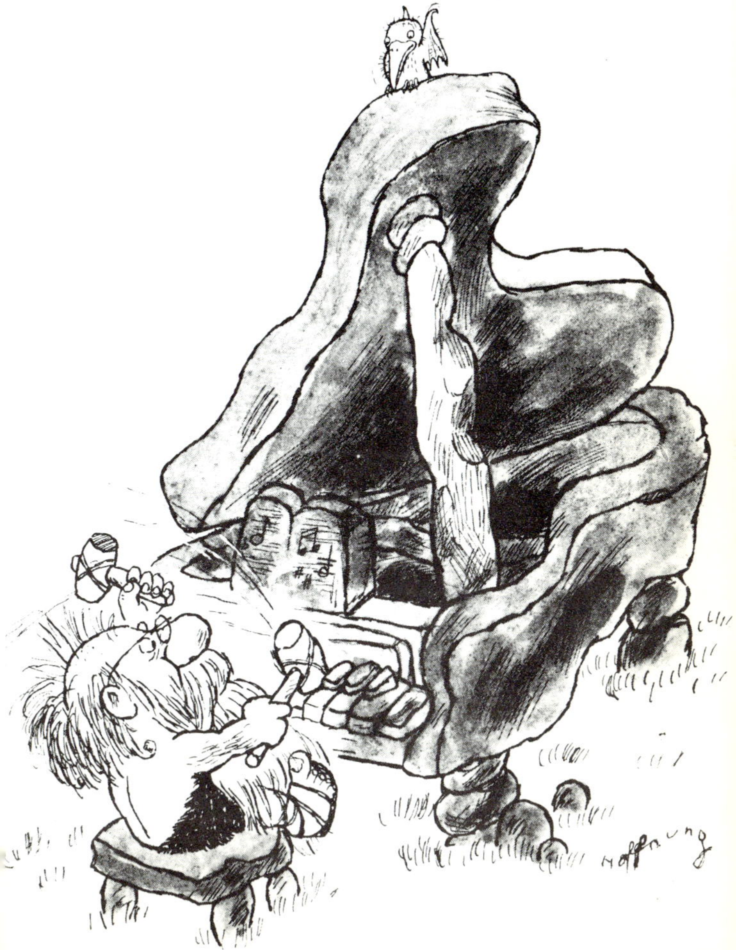
Hoffnung

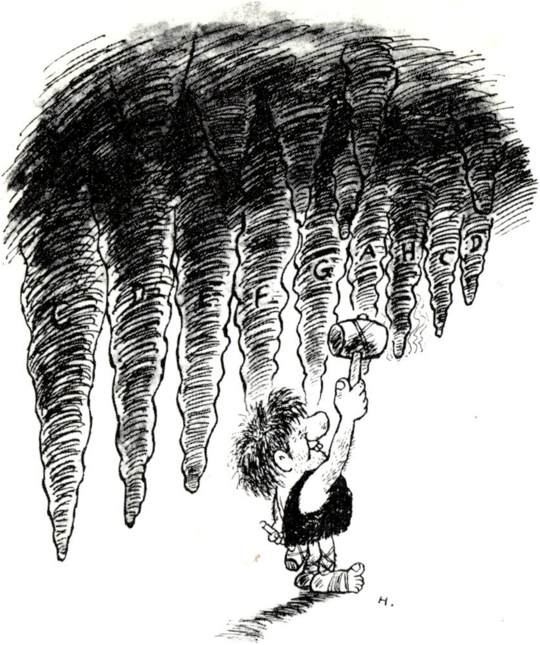
C D E F G A H C D
H.

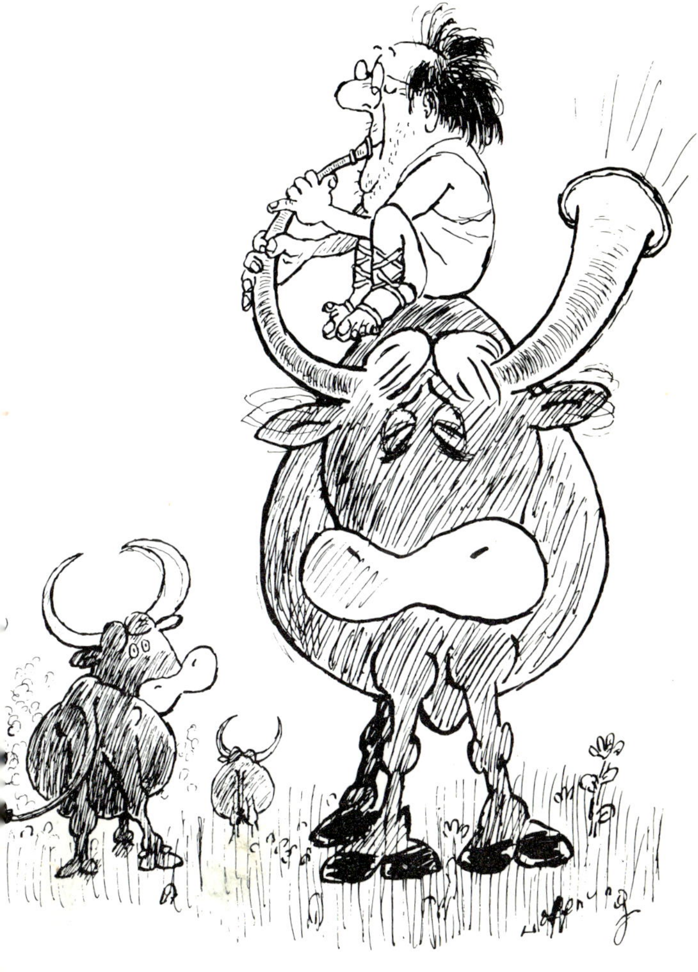

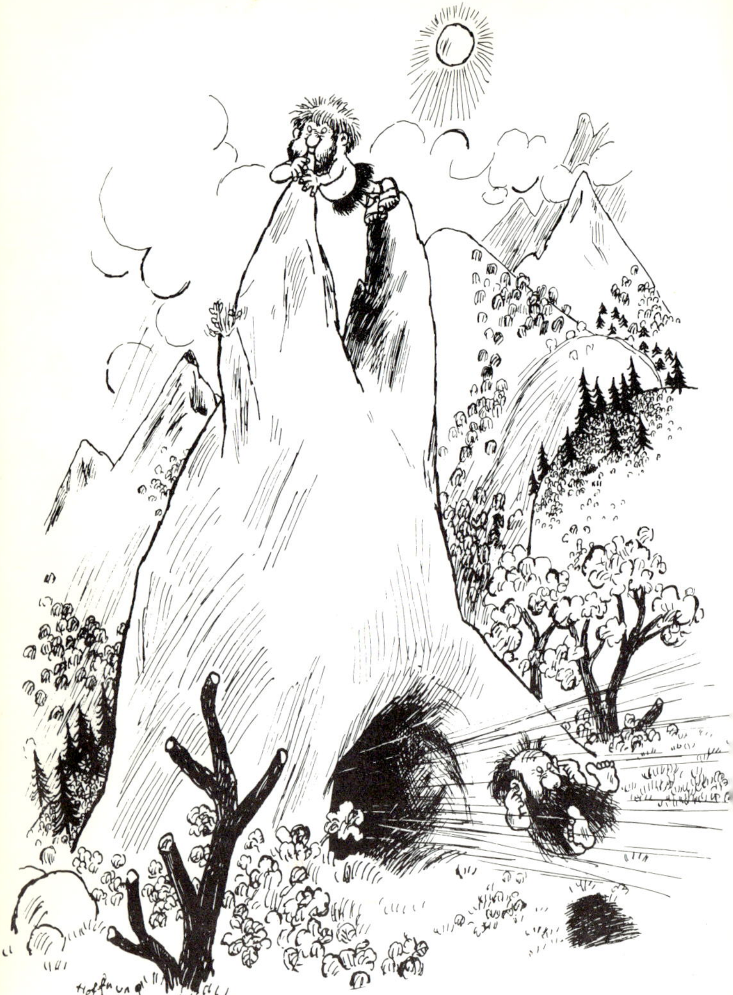
Hoffnung

Mountain-horn (in E flat)

A Chapel in the Valley

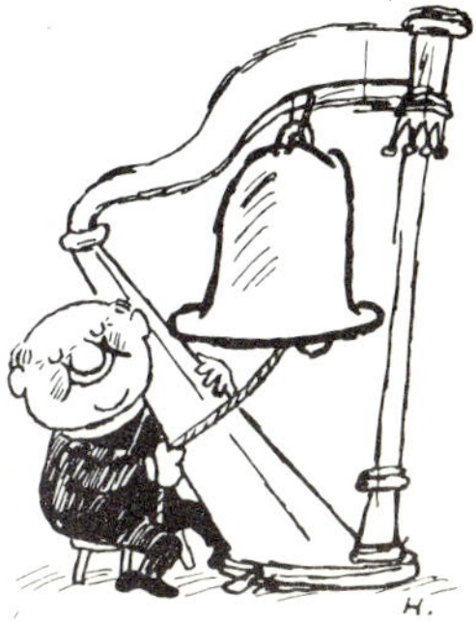

H.

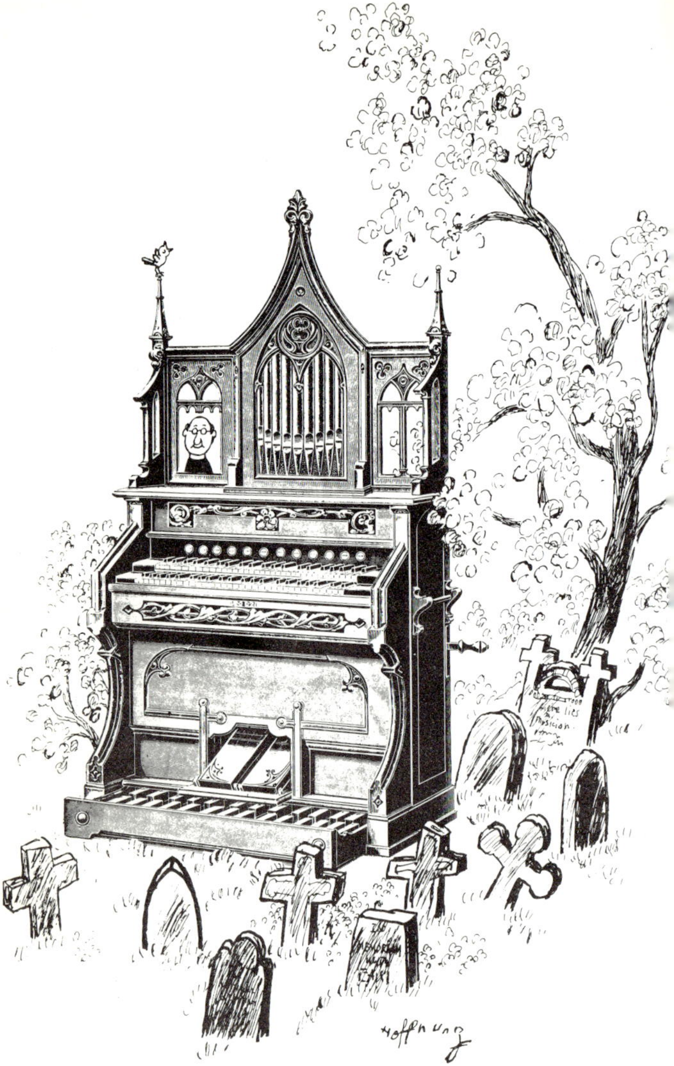
Here lies a Musician
Hoffnung

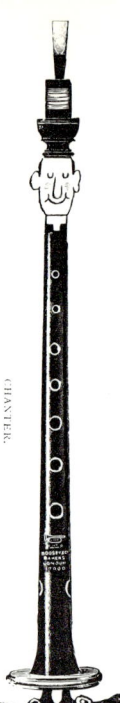

CHANTER.

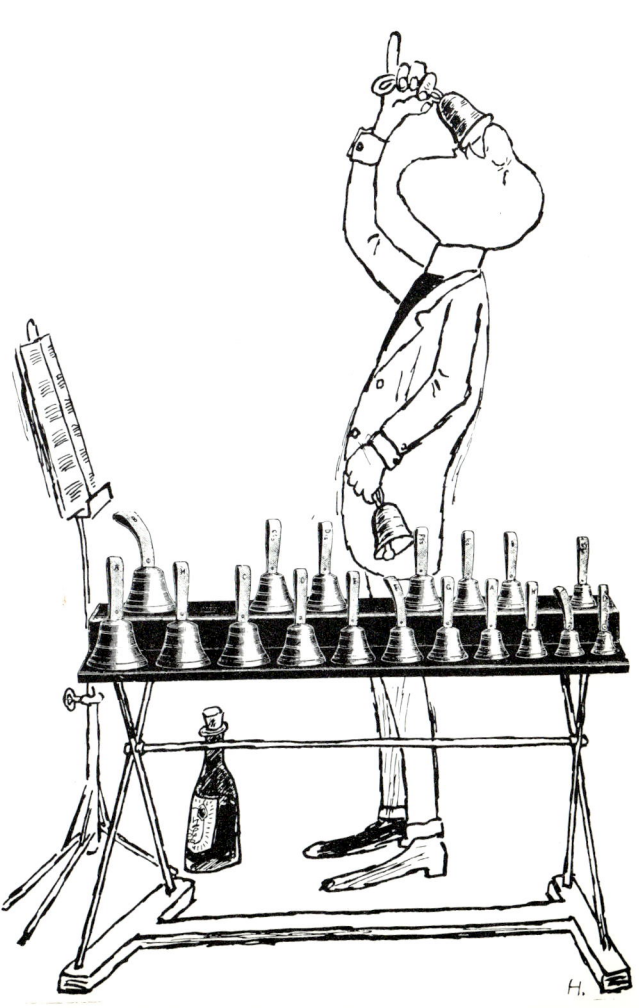

Marche Funèbre

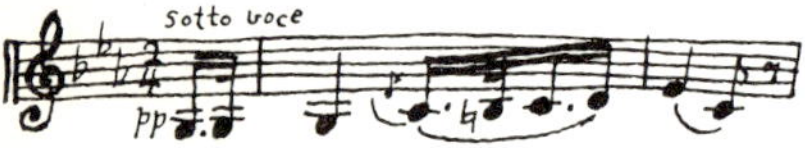
sotto voce
pp

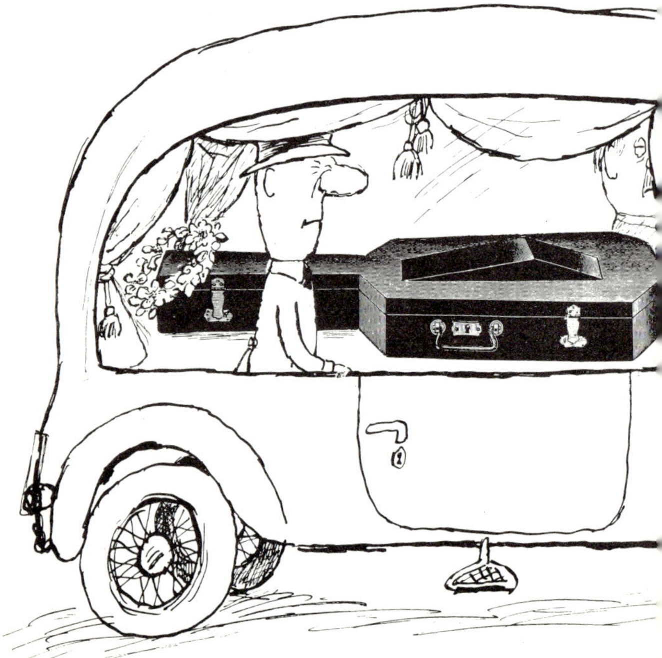

Symphonia Domestica

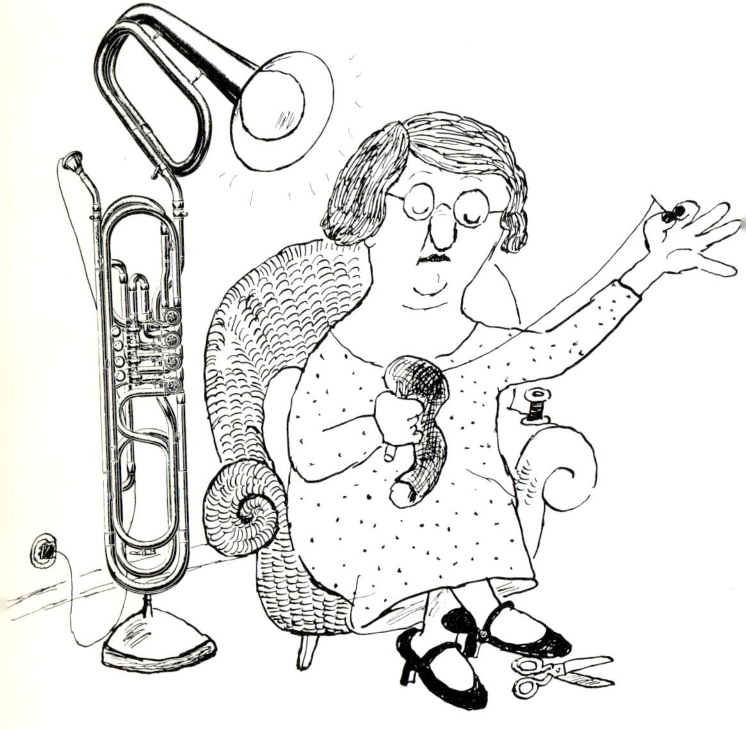

H.

H.

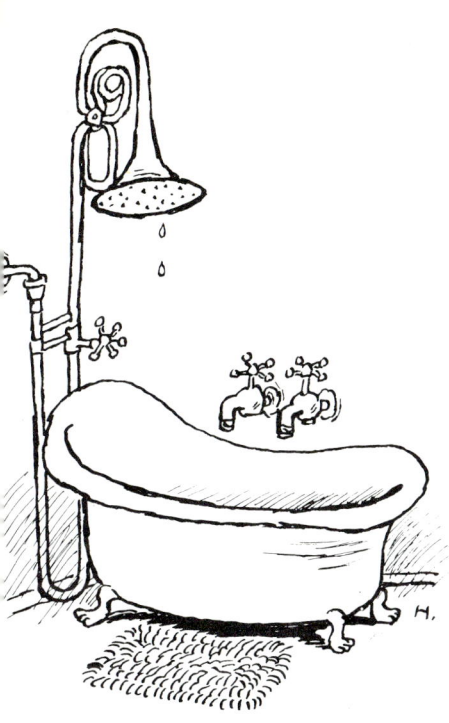

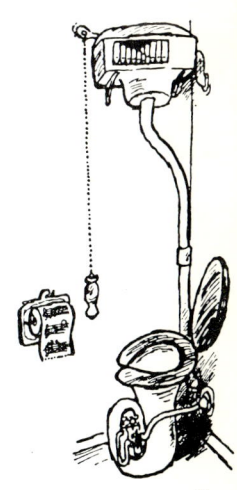

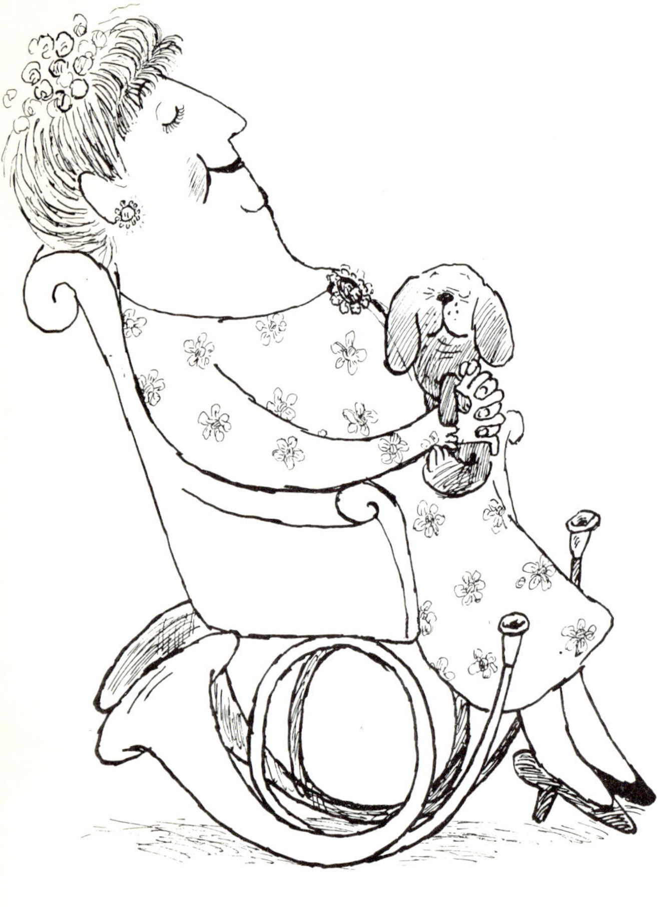

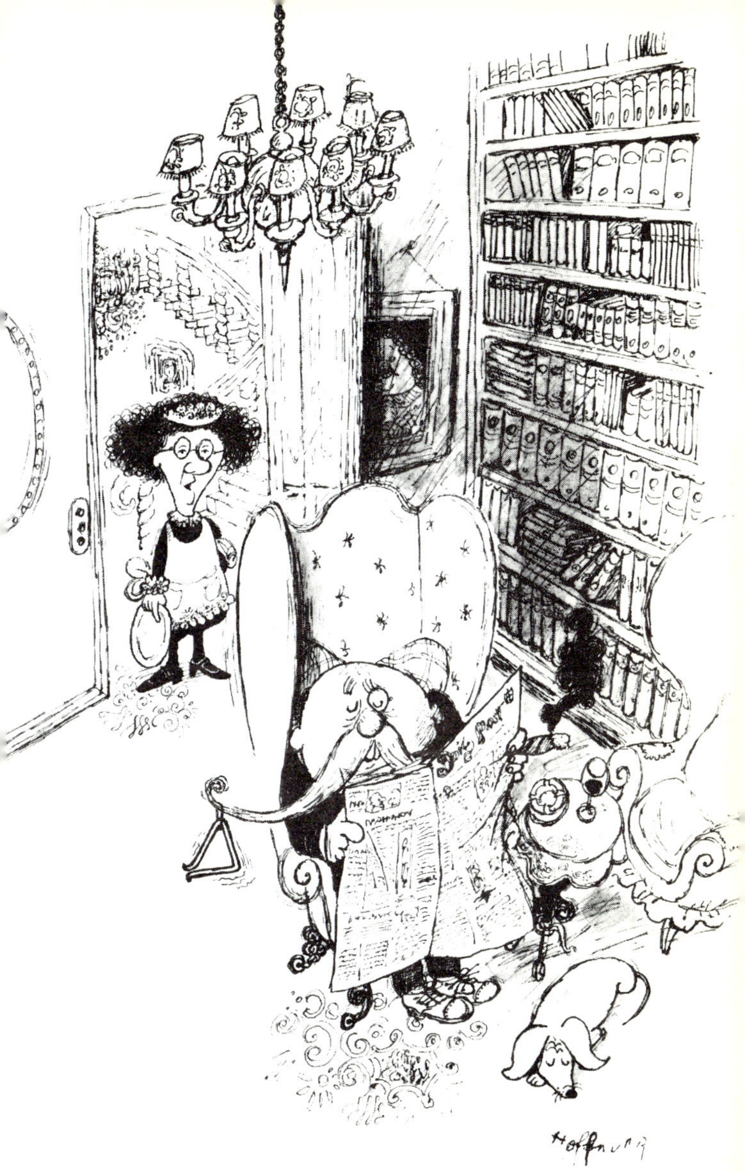

"Did you ring Sir?"

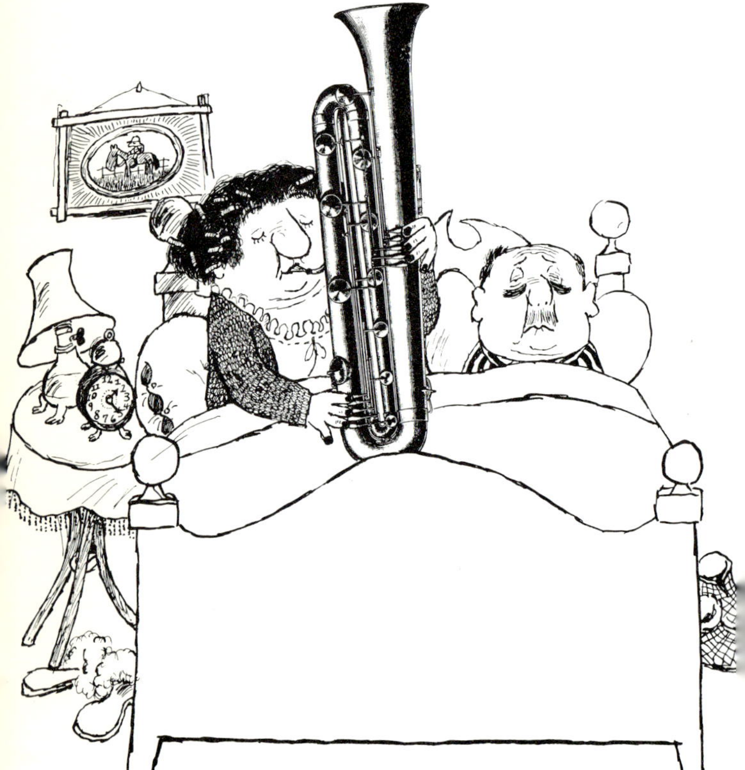

Children's Corner

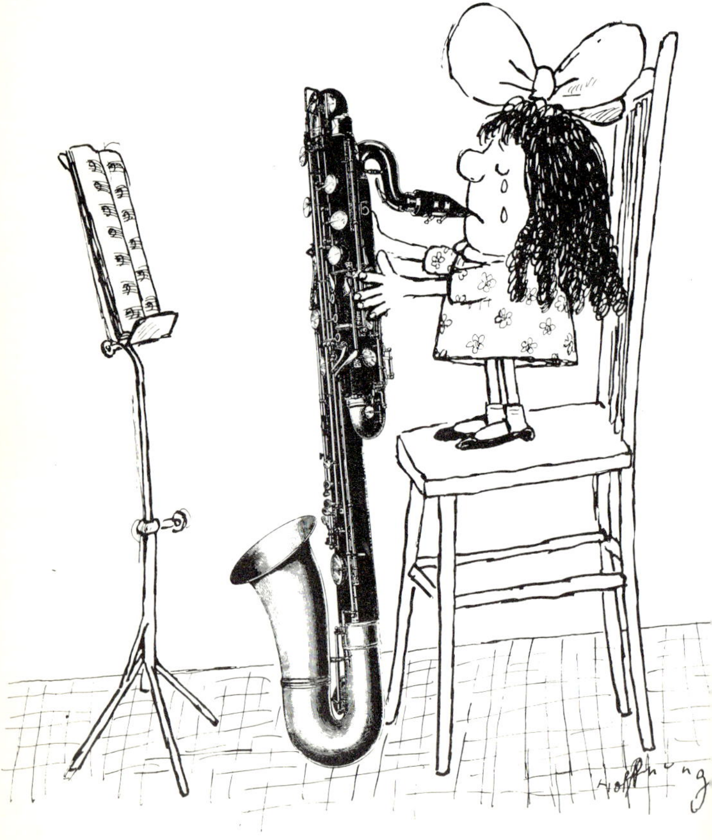

Impromptu à la mode

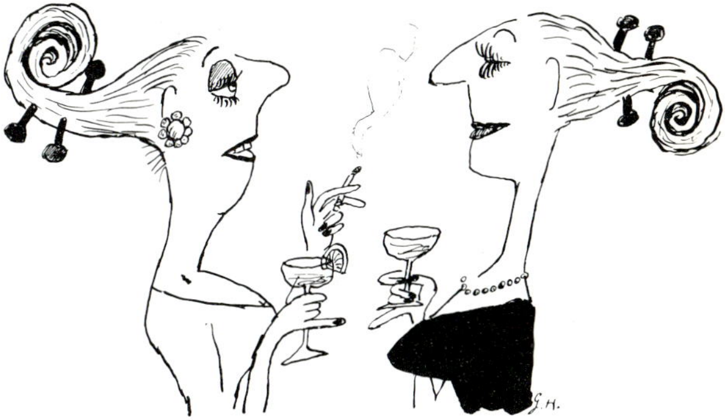
G.H.

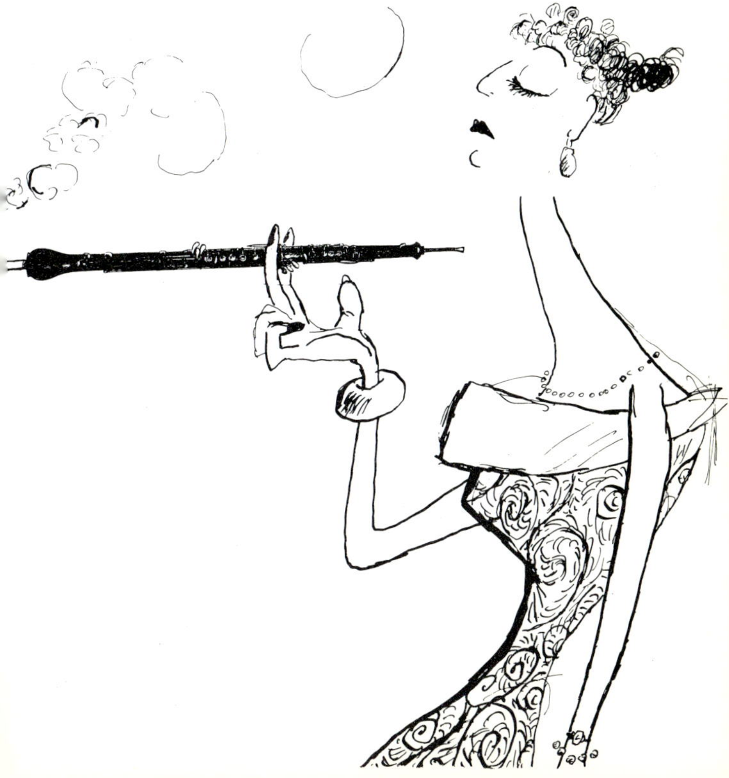

The Trumpet Shall Sound

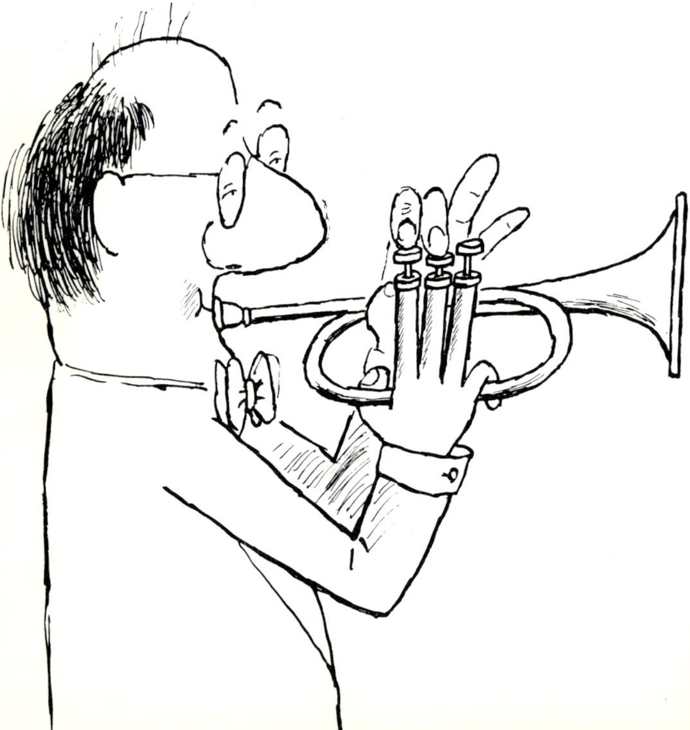

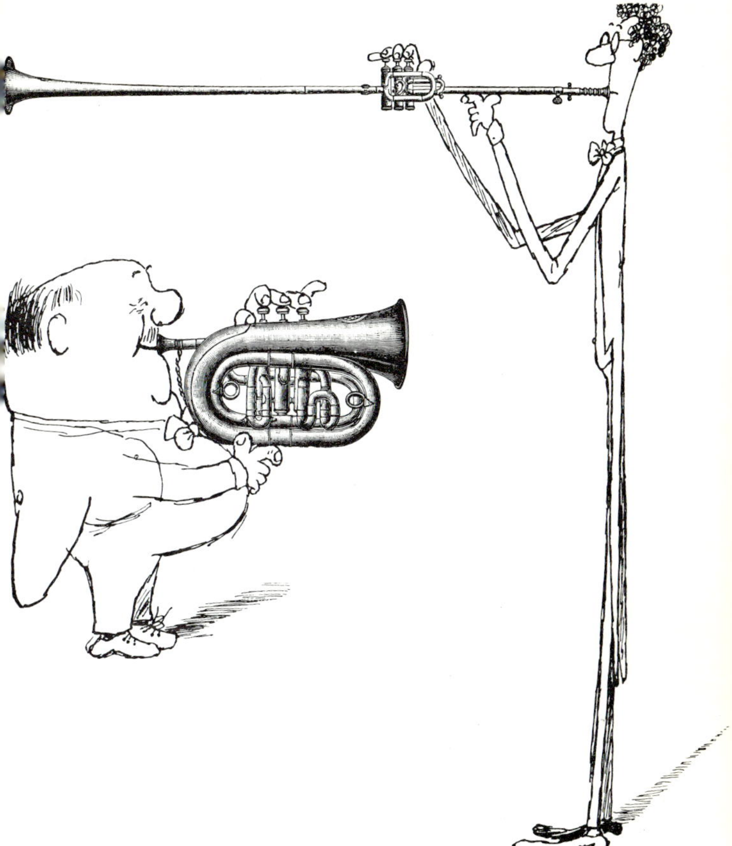

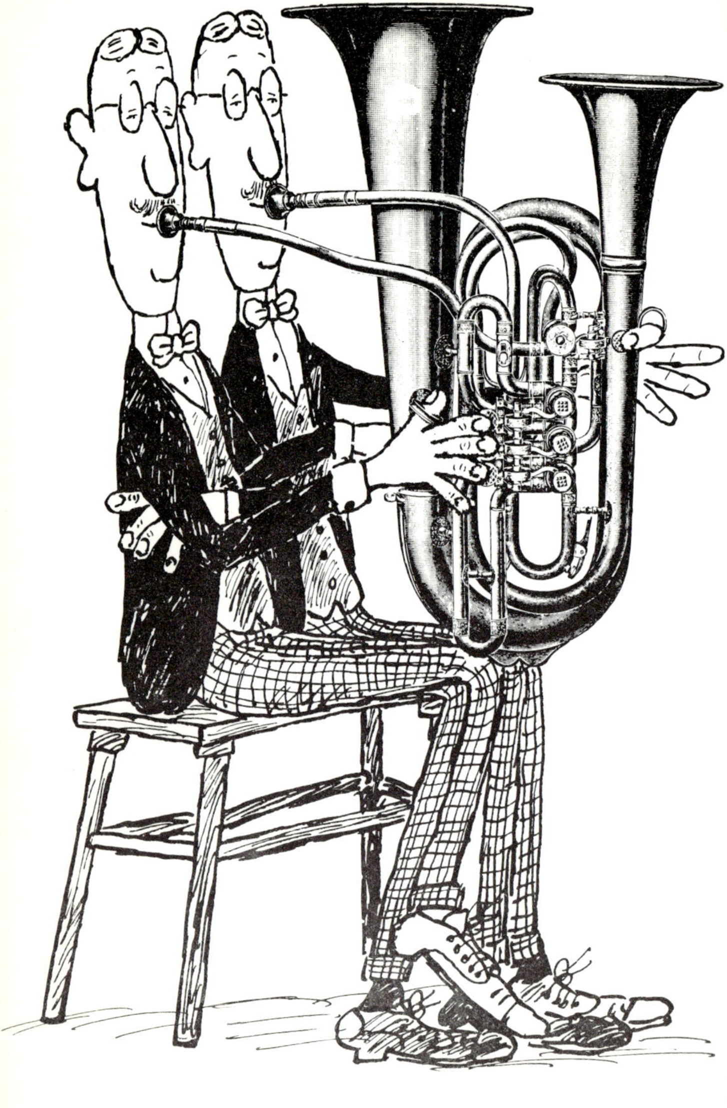

Allegro con spirito

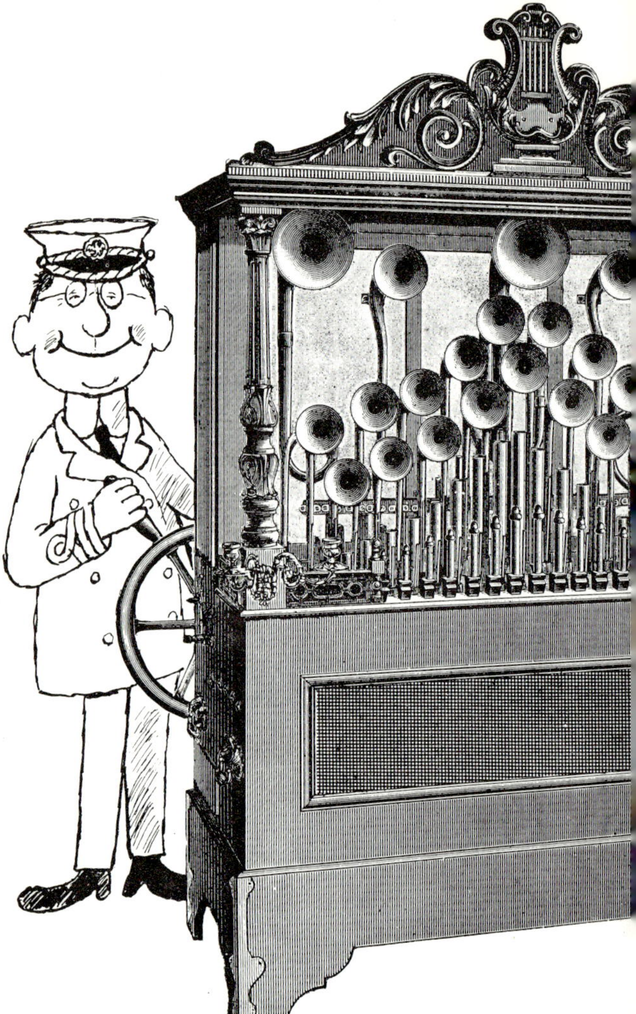

Calm Sea and a Prosperous Voyage

Postlude

1.

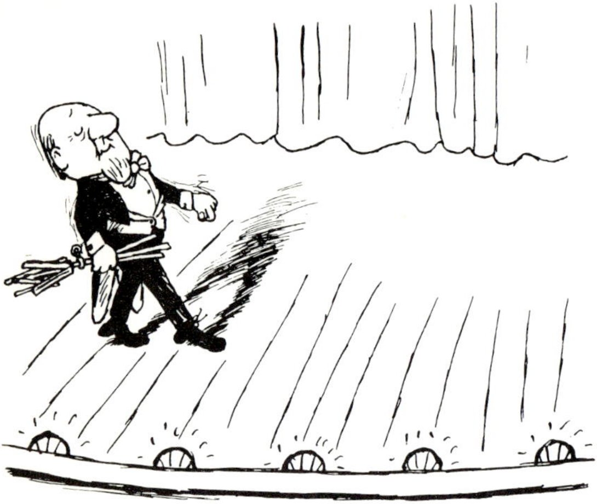

2.

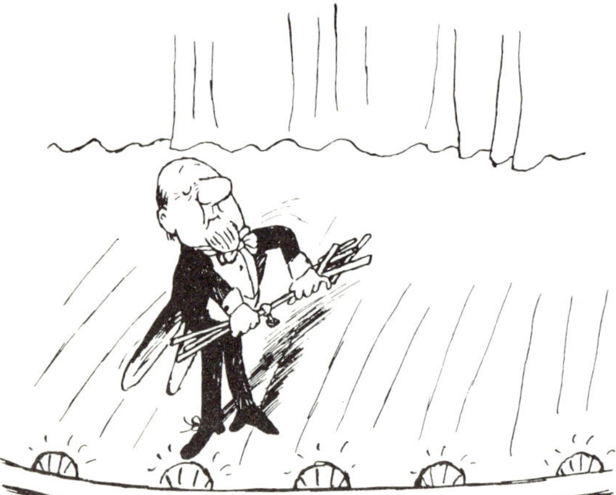

5.

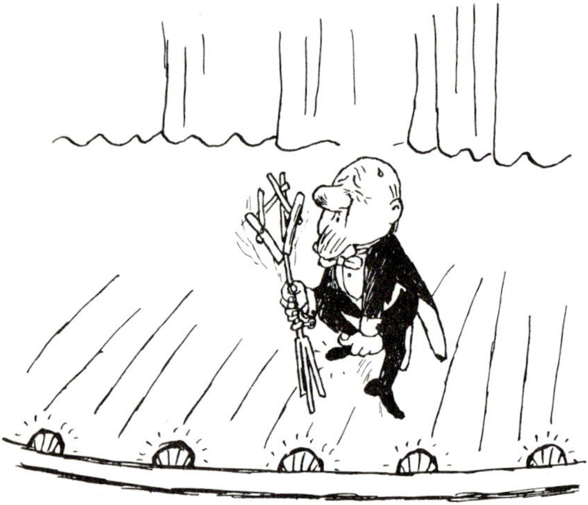

6.

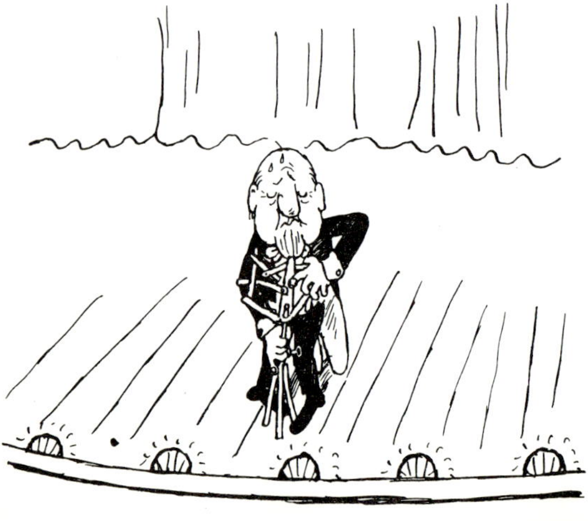

7.

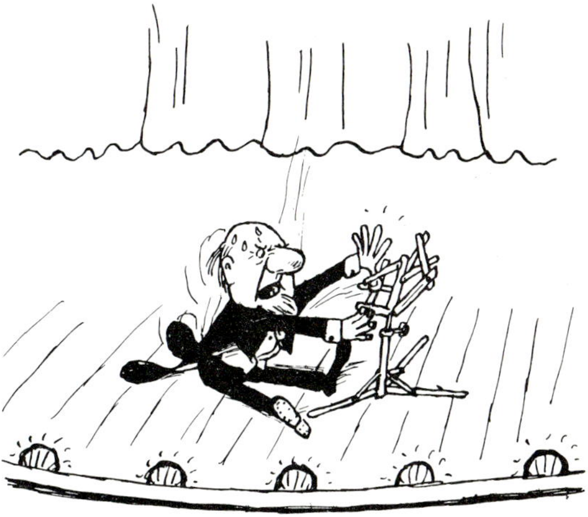

8.

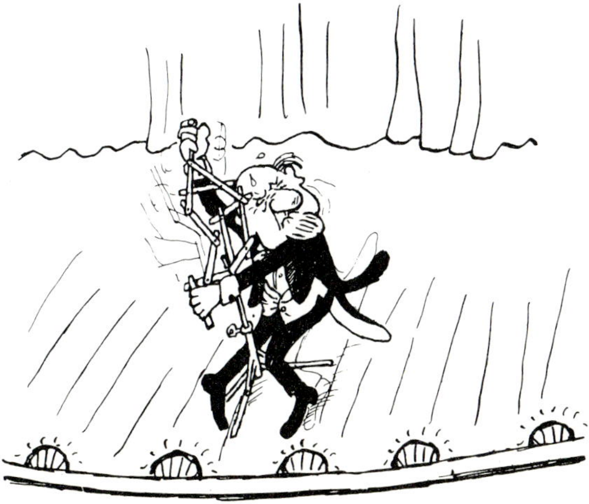

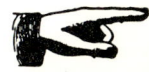

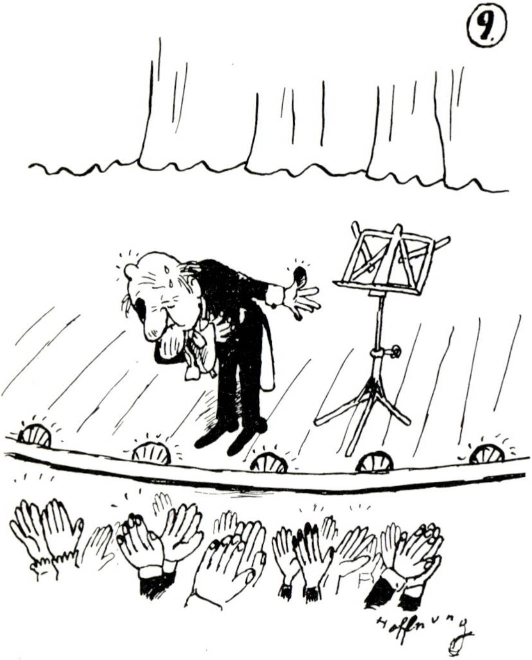
9.
Hoffnung

THE END.